{ Little-Known
FACTS
ABOUT
Well-Known
PLACES }

NEW YORK

{ *Little-Known* FACTS ABOUT *Well-Known* PLACES }

NEW YORK

DAVID HOFFMAN

METRO BOOKS
NEW YORK

Images by: Clipart.com

Metro Books
122 Fifth Avenue
New York, NY 10011

ISBN: 978-1-4351-0430-3

Printed and bound in the United States of America

1   3   5   7   9   10   8   6   4   2

INTRODUCTION

Italy, Paris, New York...just hear their names and dozens of familiar images come to mind. But for everything that we may know about these (and other) favorite places, there is always a tidbit, a top secret, or a twist of fate that we have yet to discover.

Little-Known Facts about Well-Known Places goes beyond the obvious to reveal the stories behind the stories regarding the cities, countries, and tourist destinations that we all are familiar with—or at least think we're familiar with.

Covering every aspect—from food, film, and fashion to people, history, art, and architecture—these collections of offbeat facts and figures, statistics and specifics, are guaranteed to delight a first-time visitor and surprise even the most jaded local.

Packed with a wealth of revelations that could start (or stop) a conversation—not to mention win a ton of bar bets—*Little-Known Facts about Well-Known Places* is a must-have for know-it-alls, information addicts, curious readers, armchair travelers, and pop culture junkies of all ages.

Look for these other
titles in the series

{ *Little-Known*
FACTS
ABOUT
Well-Known
PLACES }

ITALY

PARIS

DISNEYLAND

IRELAND

One explanation for New York's nickname "the Big Apple" goes like this: In the 1920s, there were four important racetracks in and around New York City with a fifth upstate in Saratoga. To the stable boys who followed horses on the circuit up and down the east coast, New York was the big time, and they took to calling it "the Big Apple." Credit for popularizing the name goes to 1920s newspaperman John FitzGerald, who covered horseracing for the *Morning Telegraph* in a column he dubbed "Around the Big Apple."

he red star in the Macy's logo
was taken from a tattoo on founder
R.H. Macy's hand—one he got as a
teenager while working on a
Nantucket whaling ship.

The only real person to ever be depicted as a balloon in the Macy's Thanksgiving Day Parade was singer and comedian Eddie Cantor.

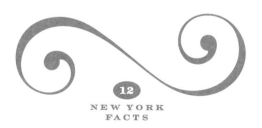

Macy's flagship store at Herald Square is, as billed, the largest store in the world, with over 2,000,000 square feet of floor space.

The first incarnation of Tiffany & Co. was as a stationery and fancy goods store that opened in September of 1837.

$4.98

Total sales on Tiffany's opening day

128.54 CARATS

weight of the "Fancy Yellow" Tiffany
diamond on display in the New York
City store on Fifth Avenue

Brooks Brothers, founded in New York in 1818, tailored uniforms for Union officers during the Civil War and custom-made the coat Abraham Lincoln wore for his second inauguration in 1865—the same coat he was wearing just a few weeks later, when he was assassinated.

When a woman walked into Abercrombie & Fitch looking for the gambling game she had played in China, co-founder Ezra Fitch tracked one down, liked what he saw, and then proceeded to send emissaries to Chinese villages to buy every set they could find. Within weeks, the 12,000 mah-jongg games he had imported had sold out and a national craze had begun.

Ubiquitous New York drugstore chain Duane Reade got its name because its first store was located on Broadway, in Tribeca, between Duane and Reade streets.

The Titanic
was supposed to
dock at Chelsea Piers,
its final destination,
on April 16, 1912.

Although long associated with Radio City Music Hall, the world-famous Rockettes actually formed in St. Louis, and were known as the Missouri Rockets before moving east.

To create the impression that all of the Rockettes are the same height, the tallest women dance in the middle of the line, and the shorter women stay on the ends. Their skirts are different lengths, altered so that the bottoms hems form a straight line, which further perpetuates the illusion.

5 FEET, 6 INCHES
minimum height to be a Rockette

5 FEET, 10½ INCHES
maximum height to be a Rockette

36
Rockettes in the dance line

200
"eye-high" kicks performed each show

9
costume changes per show

The original red and white wooden soldier uniform worn by the Rockettes during the Radio City Christmas Spectacular was designed by Vincente Minnelli, who was Radio City's art director before becoming an Academy Award-winning film director.

65,000

people who work in Rockefeller Center

175,000

people who visit Rockefeller Center
daily for business or pleasure

60

cities in the United States whose
population is greater than the daily
population (240,000) of
Rockefeller Center

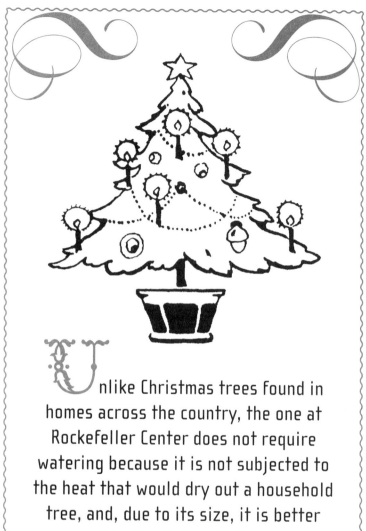

nlike Christmas trees found in homes across the country, the one at Rockefeller Center does not require watering because it is not subjected to the heat that would dry out a household tree, and, due to its size, it is better able to retain moisture.

30,000

energy-efficient LED lights, on 5 miles of wire, used to decorate the tree

25,000

Swarovski crystals on the star at the top of the tree

100 FEET

height of the 1999 tree, the tallest Rockefeller Center Christmas tree to date

20

people (plus one 80-ton crane) needed to erect the tree

The tree in Rockefeller Center comes down two weeks after Christmas, and is then recycled. The mulch (all three tons of it) is donated to the Boy Scouts to create forest paths and prevent soil erosion while the trunk either goes to the U.S. Equestrian Team to be used as a jump or is cut into lumber for Habitat for Humanity.

The 185-foot steel spire that crowns the Chrysler Building was built in secrecy, and not hoisted on top until it was too late for the sky-scraper at 40 Wall Street that was being constructed at the same time to be changed. Thus the Chrysler Build-ing was assured of being the "world's tallest building"—at least until two years later, when the Empire State Building opened.

Half of all the world's skyscrapers of fifty stories or more are in New York City.

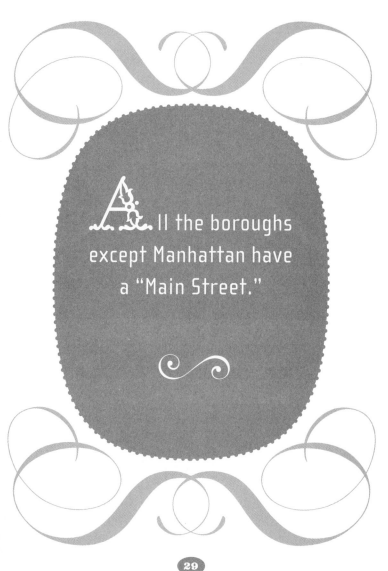

All the boroughs except Manhattan have a "Main Street."

10 MILLION
bricks in the Empire State Building

73
elevators in the Empire State Building

45 SECONDS
time it takes to ride the elevator from the lobby to the 80th floor of the Empire State Building

410 DAYS
time it took to build the Empire State Building

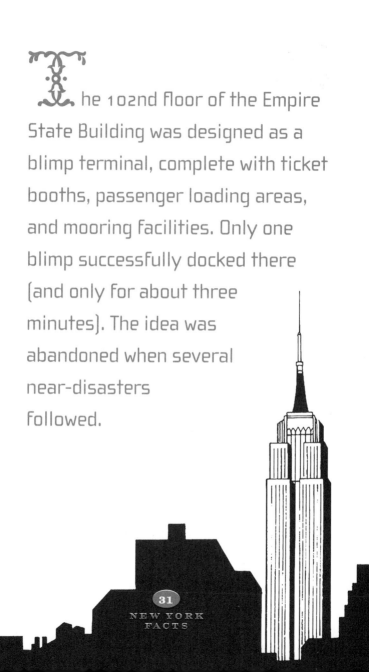

The 102nd floor of the Empire State Building was designed as a blimp terminal, complete with ticket booths, passenger loading areas, and mooring facilities. Only one blimp successfully docked there (and only for about three minutes). The idea was abandoned when several near-disasters followed.

No penny thrown from the top of the Empire State Building has ever killed anyone walking below; the building has an updraft, so a coin dropped from the observation deck would either be substantially slowed or blown by wind gusts back up against the structure, where it would most likely land on the 81st floor balcony.

On foggy nights during spring and fall migration seasons, the lights that illuminate the top thirty stories of the Empire State Building are occasionally turned off so that birds do not become disoriented by the bright lights and fly into the building.

Liberty Island is overseen by the National Parks Service and is part of New York, but technically, due to a unique interstate agreement that dates back to 1834, the actual Statue of Liberty monument stands in New Jersey waters, and hence the New Jersey address.

354

steps to the top of the
Statue of Liberty

305 FEET, 1 INCH

height of the Statue of Liberty from
the ground to the tip of the flame

879

shoe size of the Statue of Liberty,
based on the standard formula

3 FEET

width of the Statue of
Liberty's smile

The wife of French sculptor Frederic-Auguste Bartholdi spent long hours posing for the Statue of Liberty figure, but the model for the face was the artist's mother, Charlotte Bartholdi.

The angel on top of the Cathedral of St. John the Divine was the creation of sculptor John Gutzon Borglum, best known as the designer of Mt. Rushmore.

Patience and Fortitude, the two lions outside the main branch of the New York Public Library, were carved by the Piccirilli family in their South Bronx studio, where they also carved the figure of Abraham Lincoln that sits in the Lincoln Memorial in Washington, D.C.

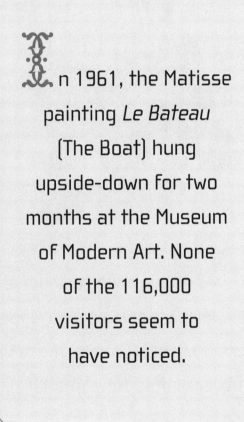

In 1961, the Matisse painting *Le Bateau* (The Boat) hung upside-down for two months at the Museum of Modern Art. None of the 116,000 visitors seem to have noticed.

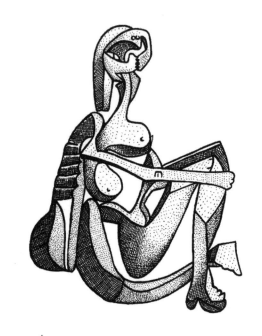

Although the Museum of Modern Art houses over 230 works by Pablo Picasso, the artist never visited New York City.

The car showroom—now a Mercedes-Benz dealership—at 56th Street and Park Avenue was designed by Frank Lloyd Wright. It holds just five vehicles, but they are dramatically displayed on a circular, sloping ramp, an architectural element that Wright would repeat later in grander form in his only other building in Manhattan, the Guggenheim Museum.

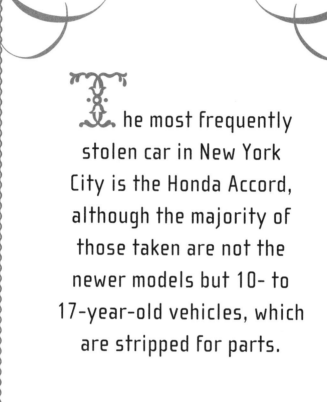

The most frequently stolen car in New York City is the Honda Accord, although the majority of those taken are not the newer models but 10- to 17-year-old vehicles, which are stripped for parts.

The first crosswalk lines anywhere were painted in New York City in 1911. Today, the crosswalks as well as lines to delineate traffic lanes are not painted; rather, they are made of a reflective white plastic that is heated to 500 degrees, then spread by machine onto the pavement, where it dries in about five minutes.

A white half-moon is painted on every subway car axle so that transit system authorities observing operations can easily detect that all of the trains' wheels are rolling.

With a fleet of more than 6,000 cars, New York City subways carry an average of nearly 5 million passengers per week and 1.5 *billion* passengers each year.

48 MPH

fastest speed a subway travels;
average speed is between
30 and 40 mph

8,872,244

passengers who rode the New
York City subway system on the
busiest day in its history
(December 23, 1946)

10 SECONDS

minimum time doors remain open
after the subway stops at a station

The "bing bong" that signals the closing of subway car doors is, musically speaking, a "descending major third"— the interval between the notes E and C. The interval is similar to that used in standard-issue doorbells and cuckoo clocks, and can be heard at the beginning of Beethoven's Fifth Symphony.

Most experienced commuters have mastered the "subway fold," a method of folding a broadsheet newspaper in half vertically, then horizontally, so that it can be read while seated or standing on the train without disturbing neighboring passengers.

Subway cars running on the lettered lines are 1 foot, 3 inches wider than the cars that run on the numbered lines.

Beneath the downtown platform at the 42nd Street/Port Authority subway station is a lower level platform once used for trains to Aqueduct Racetrack. Now the platform is leased by the Metropolitan Transportation Authority to film companies shooting New York subway scenes.

Establishing shots of the courthouse on the TV series *Law & Order* depict the building at 60 Centre Street in Manhattan. Yes, it is a courthouse, but in reality, it only contains those courtrooms where New York City's civil cases are heard. The venue for criminal cases (similar to those featured on the show) is the Criminal Courts Building, two blocks away, at 100 Centre Street.

 ccording to composer Mike Post, the distinctive *ching-ching* that plays over scene changes on *Law & Order* was made by combining a number of different sounds, including a jail door closing and a group of monks stamping on a floor.

The three-tone musical chime that identifies NBC is composed of three notes—G, E, and C—for the company's original (and current) owner, General Electric Corporation.

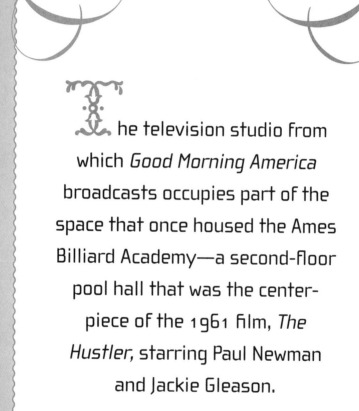

he television studio from which *Good Morning America* broadcasts occupies part of the space that once housed the Ames Billiard Academy—a second-floor pool hall that was the center-piece of the 1961 film, *The Hustler*, starring Paul Newman and Jackie Gleason.

Duke Ellington,
Frank Sinatra,
Judy Garland, and
the Beatles have
all performed at
Carnegie Hall.

$160,000

amount the Beatles were paid
for their August 15, 1965
concert at Shea Stadium

28 MINUTES

length of the Beatles'
performance at their
August 15, 1965
concert at Shea Stadium

Although he was two years away from becoming a Monkee (and a pop sensation in his own right), Davy Jones appeared on *The Ed Sullivan Show* the same night that the Beatles first did, February 9, 1964. He performed as the Artful Dodger in a musical number with other members of the original Broadway cast of *Oliver!*

oining Davy Jones in the original 1964 Broadway cast of *Oliver!*, performing the role of Mr. Sowerberry, the undertaker, was Barry Humphries, who is better known to theatergoers today as Dame Edna. He can be heard singing "That's Your Funeral" on the cast recording.

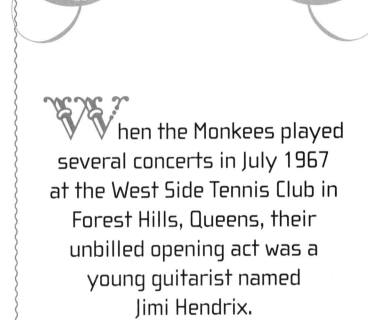

When the Monkees played several concerts in July 1967 at the West Side Tennis Club in Forest Hills, Queens, their unbilled opening act was a young guitarist named Jimi Hendrix.

At the turn of the twentieth century, the term "tin pan" was slang for an old, upright piano. The blocks on 28th Street between Fifth and Sixth avenues were lined with the offices of music publishers, each of which had a piano used to demonstrate new songs. During the summer, the sound of all those pianos would waft through open windows and resonate between buildings giving rise to the name Tin Pan Alley.

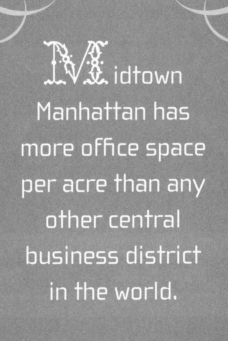

Midtown Manhattan has more office space per acre than any other central business district in the world.

23.4 MILLION
square feet of office space in the
Times Square area

1,500
businesses in Times Square

250
major billboards in Times Square

$2.5 MILLION
yearly cost to rent prime billboard
space in Times Square

he "Downtown" Petula Clark sang about in her 1960s hit is, technically speaking, midtown; composer Tony Hatch wrote the song about Times Square.

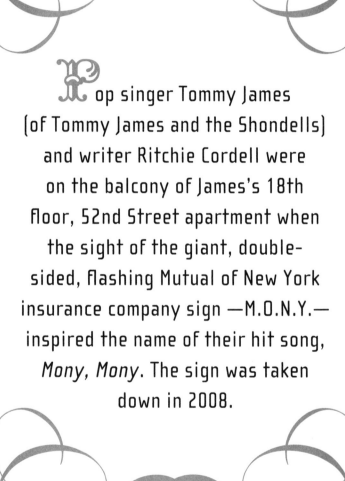

Pop singer Tommy James (of Tommy James and the Shondells) and writer Ritchie Cordell were on the balcony of James's 18th floor, 52nd Street apartment when the sight of the giant, double-sided, flashing Mutual of New York insurance company sign —M.O.N.Y.— inspired the name of their hit song, *Mony, Mony*. The sign was taken down in 2008.

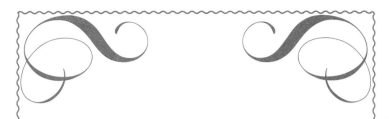

When Joni Mitchell penned the song *Chelsea Morning* she was, in fact, living in Chelsea, in a ground-floor apartment at 41 West 16th Street.

The legendary photo on the cover of *The Freewheelin' Bob Dylan* that depicts the singer in the middle of a New York City street, arm in arm with his girlfriend Suze Rotolo, was shot on Jones Street between Bleecker and West 4th streets in Greenwich Village.

A section of East 3rd Street, from Broadway to the Bowery, is known as Great Jones Street, in honor of Samuel Jones, a lawyer and politician who bequeathed land to the city in 1789 with the provision that when a road was built on it, it would be named after him. One was built, but since there was already a Jones Street in Greenwich Village, the new and wider street was named Great Jones.

The terms *jones* and *jonesing*, both slang for an intense craving or desire, originated among the heroin addicts in Great Jones Alley, off Great Jones Street, on the block between Broadway and Lafayette Street.

Immigrants arriving at Ellis Island were served ice cream as part of their first American meal. Baffled, many attempted to spread it on their bread.

A traditional Brooklyn egg cream contains neither eggs nor cream but rather seltzer, milk, and chocolate syrup.

When Horn & Hardart opened its first New York Automat on Broadway in Times Square in 1912, it only offered four items: rolls, beans, fishcakes, and coffee.

The classic blue and white, Greek-themed paper coffee cup is called the *Anthora* and was the brainchild of the Sherri Cup Company. Seeking to break into the lucrative New York City diner market, in the late 1960s the company developed the design to appeal directly to New York's many Greek-American diner owners. The gambit worked: Today, 200 million Anthora cups are sold annually.

Among the customers who regularly dined at Delmonico's (birthplace of Eggs Benedict, Lobster Newburg, and Baked Alaska) was Diamond Jim Brady, who, legend has it, sat five inches from the table and only stopped eating once his stomach touched it.

In 1926, when Italian immigrants Pio Bozzi and John Ganzi wanted to open a restaurant in Manhattan's east 40s, they planned to call it La Parma, in honor of the region they came from. A city clerk misunderstood their thick accents and mistakenly issued them a license to do business as The Palm. Rather than have the license reissued, the pair stuck with the new name.

Hector Boiardi, the former
chef of the Plaza Hotel, decided to
bottle his famous spaghetti
and meat sauce. With local
success came an offer for national
distribution, but, fearing that
Americans would have trouble
pronouncing his Italian surname, he
marketed and sold his tasty treat
under the phonetic spelling,
"Boy-ar-dee."

In 1975, while on vacation with friends, Sirio Maccioni, the owner of Le Cirque on Manhattan's East Side, improvised a dish using what he had on hand—spaghetti, spring vegetables, frozen peas, and cream—and called it Pasta Primavera. When fellow traveler and *New York Times* food columnist Craig Claiborne waxed passionate over it in the paper, customers bombarded Le Cirque demanding the dish. Maccioni added it to the menu, where it remains a staple.

According to the New York City Health Department, pizzerias are not allowed to leave a cooked pie sitting out and displayed on the counter for longer than two hours.

The kitchen at the
Waldorf-Astoria Hotel
in midtown Manhattan
has a meat locker
with its own security
system.

An unbelievably rude waiter at Oscar's Tavern so amused Muppet creator Jim Henson and *Sesame Street* director Jon Stone that he inspired the creation of Oscar the Grouch.

All of the Broadway shows depicted in the framed theater posters that line the walls of Joe Allen Restaurant were notorious flops.

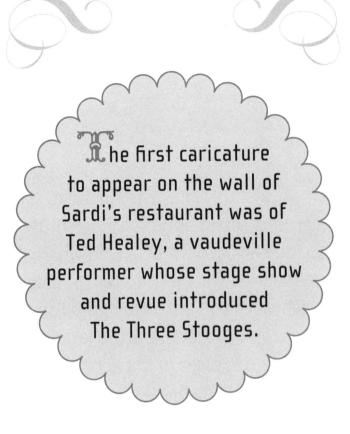

The first caricature to appear on the wall of Sardi's restaurant was of Ted Healey, a vaudeville performer whose stage show and revue introduced The Three Stooges.

Alex Gard, the Russian refugee hired by Vincent Sardi to do caricatures of Broadway celebrities for his theater district restaurant, was never paid for his work. Instead, Gard chose to do the drawings in exchange for meals.

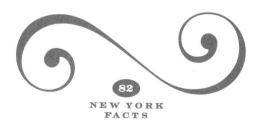

1,300
caricatures on display at Sardi's

18,696
approximate number of eating establishments in New York City, not including food trucks

$39.43
average cost of a dinner in New York City in 2006 (drink, tax, and tip included), according to the Zagat Survey

In addition to its regular menu, Sardi's has a lower-priced Actors' Menu for anyone (and a guest) who is a member of one of the three actor's unions (Equity, SAG, or AFTRA). Instituted by Vincent Sardi to help struggling performers, the discounts are even better on Wednesdays when the already reduced prices are cut in half.

 chicken and egg dish, called "Mother and Child Reunion," on the menu at Say Eng Look (a former restaurant on East Broadway in Chinatown) gave Paul Simon the inspiration and title for his hit song which, for the record, is actually about the death of a beloved family dog.

he folded white cardboard cartons with wire handles commonly used by Chinese restaurants for takeout and delivery were developed in 1900 as pails to carry freshly opened oysters packed in ice.

100 MILLION
Chinese food cartons used
annually in New York City

60
ashtrays stolen daily from
the Stork Club on East 53rd
Street during its heyday
in the 1950s

12,000
number of bagels sold each
weekend at Zabar's on
Manhattan's Upper West Side

The term "86-ed," meaning to toss out or refuse to serve a customer, reportedly owes its origins to Chumley's, a former bar in Greenwich Village. During speakeasy days, the management would toss out unruly customers, forcing them to leave via the unmarked door, at 86 Bedford Street.

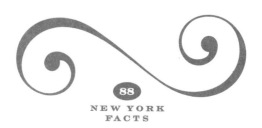

McSorley's Old Ale House on East 7th Street, which opened in 1854, is one of the oldest bars in Manhattan and has served only one beverage in its long history: McSorley's Ale (dark or light). Because of its "beer only" license, McSorley's was allowed to remain open during Prohibition, which made it, at that time, the only legal bar in the country.

(Legal maybe, but also sexist: McSorley's did not admit women until August 1970.)

athan Handwerker opened Nathan's Famous in Coney Island in 1916 and immediately angered the competition by selling franks for a nickel when everyone else was charging a dime. To dispel rumors that his franks contained horsemeat to keep prices low, Handwerker dressed several young men in white lab coats and stethoscopes and paid them to stand around his place chowing down on free hot dogs. When word spread that "doctors" ate at Nathan's, business flourished.

The first roller coaster in the world was built at Coney Island in 1884.

Coney Island's popularity inspired piano manufacturer William Steinway to open a similar retreat on the Queens shoreline. Despite the initial success of his Bowery Bay Beach, attendance thinned during World War I and stopped completely during Prohibition. The structures were torn down, a portion of the bay was filled in, and a tiny airport was built. Several years, hundreds of millions of dollars, and a handful of name changes later, it became known as LaGuardia Airport.

Construction of the Sixth Avenue subway (the "F" line) began in 1934, and included demolition of the elevated train tracks that had been in use since the late 1800s. As part of the redesign, Mayor Fiorello LaGuardia lined the avenue with arched streetlamps, each bearing a large circular medallion representing a different country in North, South, or Central America. Thus, Sixth Avenue took on a new name: "Avenue of the Americas."

By the Numbers

44 MILLION
annual visitors to New York City
(7 million international)

60
languages spoken by licensed New
York City taxi drivers

85
nationalities of licensed
New York City taxi drivers

100 MILLION
Americans (roughly 40 percent of the
population) whose relatives entered
the U.S. through Ellis Island

There are more Irish people in New York City than in any other city in the world; the same goes for Jews, Puerto Ricans, and Dominicans. Additionally, there are more Brazilians in New York City than in any area outside South America, more Greeks than in any city outside Greece, and more Chinese than in any city outside Asia.

While the United Nations sits squarely on the east side of Manhattan, the land it occupies is an international zone with its own postal service, fire department, and security force.

Central Park comprises its own United States census tract (number 143, to be exact), and according to the last report, the park's population was 18 persons (12 male, six female) with a median age of 38.5 years.

$528,783,552,000

estimated real estate value of
Central Park

843 ACRES

size of Central Park

51

sculptures in Central Park

29

maximum number of model boats
allowed on Conservatory Water
(the Central Park sailboat pond)

The lampposts in Central Park not only light the way, they tell you where you are. Most are marked with numbers; the first two or three digits identify which cross street you would be on, if that street ran straight through the park. The letter W, C, or E alongside the numbers indicates whether you are in the western, central, or eastern part of the park.

Two male penguins at the Central Park Zoo were engaged in a stable long-term relationship for six years. When zookeepers noticed they were trying to hatch a rock, they entrusted them with an extra penguin egg from another pair and the boys did a good job: Tango, a female, was born approximately five weeks later.

Despite weathering the elements (not to mention the pigeons) for over eighty years, the statue of Balto (the famous Siberian Husky sled dog from the 1920s who inspired the Iditarod) that sits in Central Park has a perpetually polished appearance thanks to visitors who pet it as if it were a real dog.

530,000
dogs in New York City

1,787
residents 100 years
of age or older in
New York City

11,000 TONS
amount of garbage
New York City generates
in one day

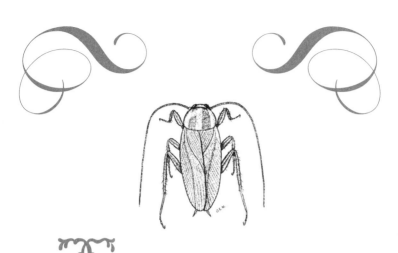

The cockroach most common in New York City apartments is the German cockroach; the most prevalent rat is the Norwegian rat.

Once a common type of residence, the "walk-up" is slowly vanishing from the New York City landscape and lexicon, due to the fact that, since 1987, any new residential building of more than two stories is required by law to have an elevator.

In 1880, when Edward Clark began construction on a luxury apartment complex at 72nd Street and Central Park West, he was ridiculed for his choice of location. Naysayers joked that it was so far from desired residential areas it might as well be in the Dakota Territory. Undeterred, Clark not only had his architect add Dakotan emblems, including cornstalks, arrowheads, and a figure of a Native American to the design, he named his building the Dakota.

By opening day, all of the apartments at the Dakota had been rented. It remains one of New York City's most esteemed addresses, and, over the years, everyone from Judy Garland to John Lennon to Leonard Bernstein—not to mention Boris Karloff, Lauren Bacall, Carson McCullers, Rudolph Nureyev, Judy Holliday, and Gilda Radner—have called it home. Among potential residents that the board didn't approve: musicians Gene Simmons and Billy Joel.

he Ricardos' address in the TV series *I Love Lucy* was 623 East 68th Street, however the highest address number on East 68th Street in Manhattan is 600 which means (at least technically) that the Ricardos lived in the middle of the East River.

 he East River isn't actually a
river, but a tidal estuary—
an arm of the sea where salt
water meets fresh water
running off the land.

In the TV series *Seinfeld*, Jerry lived at 129 West 81st Street. That address exists in New York, but the exterior of the apartment building seen in every episode can be found at 757 New Hampshire Avenue in Los Angeles.

Coffee Shop

The restaurant exterior featured in *Seinfeld* belongs to Tom's Restaurant at West 112th Street and Broadway, the same restaurant immortalized in the Suzanne Vega song "Tom's Diner." On the show, however, the coffee shop was called Monk's—a name inspired by a poster of jazz musician Thelonious Monk in the office where Jerry Seinfeld and co-creator Larry David wrote the scripts for the show together.

Former Secretary of State Colin Powell grew up in a predominantly Jewish neighborhood in the Bronx, where he learned to speak Yiddish.

Author Washington Irving gave New York City the nickname "Gotham," in an issue of *Salmagundi*, a satirical periodical. He didn't coin it, however: Gotham is the name of a city in England where all of the residents once faked insanity to discourage the king from settling there, knowing that his taking up residence would have increased their taxes.

Of the five boroughs in New York City, Brooklyn has the most people (2.5 million); Queens is the largest in terms of area.

hen telephone area codes were first assigned, New York, the largest city in the country (and hence the one most frequently called), was given 212 because it took the least amount of time to dial on a rotary phone.

The most common surname in the New York City telephone book is Rodriguez (followed by Williams, Smith, Brown, and Rivers).

In 1959, New York City Mayor Robert Wagner called on attorney William Shea to help bring a National League baseball team back to the Big Apple after both the New York Giants and Brooklyn Dodgers moved to California. New club owner Joan Whitney Payson shortened her team's corporate name (the New York Metropolitan Baseball Club) and came up with the Mets, and, until 2008, their home field was Shea Stadium.

The team colors of the New York Mets were chosen in homage to the two teams that went before them—Brooklyn (now Los Angeles) Dodgers blue and New York (now San Francisco) Giants orange—and because blue and orange are also the colors of New York City flag.

The interlocking "NY" logo of the New York Yankees was created by Louis B. Tiffany for a Medal of Valor given by the New York City Police Department. The Yankees (then called the Highlanders) adopted it in 1909, after the team was bought by retired police chief Bill Devery.

In 1929, the New York Yankees became the first team to make numbers a permanent part of the uniform. The initial distribution of numbers was made according to the player's position in the batting order. Therefore, leadoff hitter Earle Combs wore 1; Mark Koenig, 2; Babe Ruth, 3; and Lou Gehrig, 4.

Yankees great Lou Gehrig
was the first athlete to
appear on a box of Wheaties,
"The Breakfast of Champions."

In 1926, Tex Rickard, who held the lease to promote live events at Madison Square Garden, was awarded a National Hockey League franchise. People jokingly dubbed his players "Tex's Rangers," which later evolved into the team's official name, the New York Rangers.

Madison Square Garden is neither a garden nor on Madison Square (a small park located between Fifth and Madison avenues, and 23rd and 26th streets). *Garden* was a common nineteenth century term for arenas and this one was originally on the Square; as the venue moved to new locations, the name stayed with it. The present Garden, which opened in 1968 above Penn Station between Seventh and Eighth avenues, is actually the fourth incarnation of the famed sports venue.

14 PERCENT

total land mass of New York City
that is comprised of parks
and gardens

7 HOURS, 15 MINUTES

average time it takes to swim around
the island of Manhattan

674

places in New York City on the
National Register of Historic Places
(more than any other U.S. city)

In Grand Central Station, there is a Whispering Gallery located on the lower level outside the Oyster Bar & Restaurant, where, thanks to the acoustics of the low ceramic arches, a whisper can be heard loud and clear from opposite corners of the large entryway.

In the northwest corner of the mural that spans the ceiling of the Main Concourse in Grand Central Terminal, there is a small dark patch that remains untouched. This area shows the color and condition of the ceiling prior to restoration in 1998, and was purposely left as a "before-and-after" comparison.

The zodiac depicted in the mural on the ceiling of Grand Central Terminal is backwards. Although some believe that the artist Paul Helleu made a mistake, most critics agree the perspective was deliberate, that he took his cue from a medieval manuscript that showed the heavens as if viewed from above. Whichever is correct, the plans for Grand Central Terminal had originally called for a ceiling skylight as opposed to painted stars, but that idea was scrapped when time and money ran out.

The sound of chirping birds can be heard at the Long Island Railroad waiting area in Penn Station. The birds, however, are recorded, and the sound is used to guide visually impaired travelers to an automated information booth with a talking map and telephone keypad.

In July 1978, less than a year after the Citicorp Center building was completed, William LeMessurier, a structural engineer who had consulted on the design, discovered that the bracing was abnormally susceptible to high winds and could cause the building to collapse if it were struck by a hurricane. To avoid panic, a plan was put into action to reinforce the building's joints at night, without tenants or neighbors ever knowing.

Contractions and expansions of the steel cables on the Verrazano Narrows Bridge, caused by the change in seasons, result in the double-decked roadway being twelve feet lower in the summer than it is in winter.

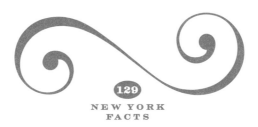

1,000,000 TONS
weight of the Verrazano
Narrows Bridge

2,027
bridges in New York City (Central
Park alone has three dozen)

21
elephants P.T. Barnum marched
across the Brooklyn Bridge in 1884
to demonstrate its stability

In an attempt to defray cost overruns after the Brooklyn Bridge was completed in 1883, a number of the underground chambers within the structure were rented for commercial use primarily as wine cellars, thanks to their consistently cool 60-degree temperatures.

The Hudson River—at least the part that runs along the west side of Manhattan—never freezes because, when necessary, the Coast Guard positions ice cutters upriver to keep the channel clear.

Each year there is a one in four chance that New York City will have a white Christmas.

In any given year, the single busiest hour in New York City is the hour between 5 and 6 p.m. on the Wednesday after Christmas due to the combination of tourists, workers, commuters, shoppers (in the stores both to return gifts and to take advantage of the after-holiday sales), and theatergoers (those leaving the matinee and those heading to an evening show).

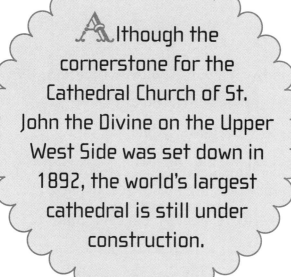

Although the cornerstone for the Cathedral Church of St. John the Divine on the Upper West Side was set down in 1892, the world's largest cathedral is still under construction.

In most Broadway theaters, the rows, which run alphabetically, traditionally jump from H to J, omitting the letter I. This is to prevent the box office, ushers, and theatergoers from confusing the letter I with the number 1, thereby reducing the odds of someone sitting in the wrong seat.

By the Numbers

39
Broadway theaters in New York City

11.2 MILLION
tickets to Broadway shows sold annually

$76.32
average ticket price for a Broadway show

$50 TO $100
amount in coins (mostly pennies) that
is collected from the reflecting pool in
front of the Vivian Beaumont Theater in
Lincoln Center every two months
(the money goes toward upkeep)

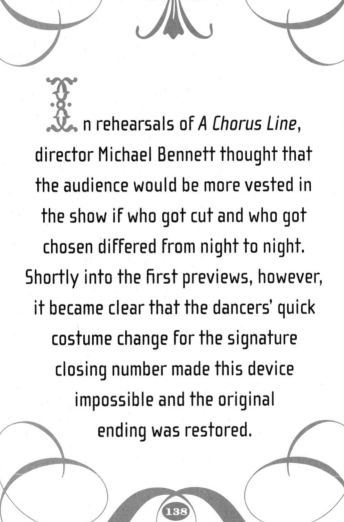

In rehearsals of *A Chorus Line*, director Michael Bennett thought that the audience would be more vested in the show if who got cut and who got chosen differed from night to night. Shortly into the first previews, however, it became clear that the dancers' quick costume change for the signature closing number made this device impossible and the original ending was restored.

In the beginning, *West Side Story* was entitled *East Side Story*, and involved an ill-fated romance between a Jewish boy and a Roman Catholic girl. Several years after the original project had been shelved, director-choreographer Jerome Robbins, composer Leonard Bernstein, and writer Arthur Laurents decided that the star-crossed love of a white boy and a Puerto Rican girl—on New York's west side—was more socially relevant, and they changed the story to suit the times.

In 1984, while a freshman in college, Cynthia Nixon not only appeared in two highly successful Mike Nichols-directed hit Broadway shows, she did so simultaneously. Nixon would perform in the first act of David Rabe's *Hurlyburly*, walk two blocks and change her costume to appear on stage in the second act of Tom Stoppard's *The Real Thing*, then walk back, change again, and resume her role in the third act of *Hurlyburly*.

According to Truman Capote, the Holly Golightly character in *Breakfast at Tiffany's* was based on his friend Carol Grace, the former wife of author William Saroyan and future wife of actor Walter Matthau.

The black Givenchy dress worn by Audrey Hepburn in the opening scenes of *Breakfast at Tiffany's* sold for $807,000 in 2006—the highest price paid, to date, for a piece of motion picture memorabilia.

In the film *The Seven-Year Itch*, the famous shot of Marilyn Monroe's dress blowing up around her legs as she stands over the subway grate was originally filmed on location at 52nd Street and Lexington Avenue. However, the noise of the crowd gathered to watch made the footage unusable so director Billy Wilder re-staged the entire scene on the 20th Century Fox movie studio lot where it required forty takes before Marilyn got her lines right.

In the late 1970s, graphic sex scenes for the porno classic *Debbie Does Dallas* were secretly filmed in the library stacks at Pratt Institute in Brooklyn, one of the most highly regarded art colleges in the country.

Thanks to an uncanny knack for getting his guests to reveal more than they ever intended (without even asking personal questions), James Lipton, founding dean of the Actor's Studio Drama School and host of TV's *Inside the Actor's Studio* has been asked by the N.Y.P.D. to coach homicide detectives in the art of interrogation.

Neil Simon's *The Goodbye Girl* began life as *Bogart Slept Here* (changed from *Gable Slept Here*) and was based on Dustin Hoffman's life as a struggling New York theater actor prior to his starring film role in *The Graduate*.

Annie Hall was originally written and shot as a Manhattan-based murder mystery, but during post-production, Woody Allen, realizing that the strongest story line was the relationship between the two main characters, re-edited the film as a romantic comedy.

efore he became the mayor of New York City Rudy Giuliani was one of the key prosecuting attorneys in the N.Y.P.D. corruption case on which the book and movie *Prince of the City* were based.

good deal of the film *Taxi Driver* was autobiographical for screenwriter Paul Schrader, who suffered a nervous break-down, developed an obsession with guns, frequented porno theaters, and did not talk to anyone for months when he first moved to Southern California in the 1970s. He set the story in Manhattan because taxi drivers were more emblematic of New York than of Los Angeles.

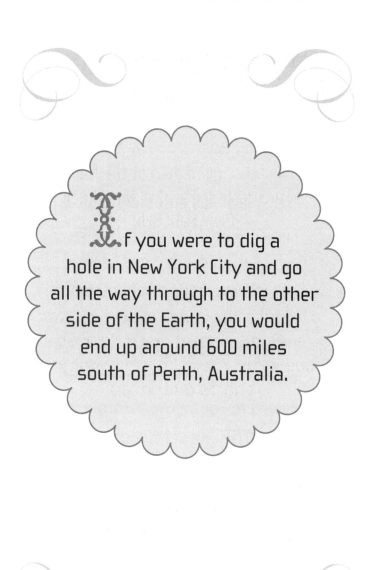

If you were to dig a hole in New York City and go all the way through to the other side of the Earth, you would end up around 600 miles south of Perth, Australia.

2.8 MILES

average length of a New York
City cab ride

$25

amount a licensed taxi driver can
be fined, according to the civil
code of New York City, for wearing
shorts on the job

$45

flat fare (not including tolls and
tip) for a ride between John F.
Kennedy International Airport
and any point in Manhattan

nly since 1968, when the City Council, wanting to cut down on unofficial drivers, issued a mandate, have all New York City taxicabs been painted yellow. Originally each fleet had its own color scheme. Yellow was selected for its visibility.

In New York City,
taxi drivers are exempt
from the law that requires
drivers to wear a seat belt
at all times.

The first police to patrol New York City had no uniforms; officers simply wore shiny metal badges on their own clothing to identify them as part of the force. According to the New York City Police Museum, the badges were made of stamped copper, so people took to calling the squad "coppers," and, in time, "cops."

Police officers in the 1870s who preferred to be assigned to the seedy midtown neighborhood running from 24th to 42nd streets, between Fifth and Seventh avenues, nicknamed it the "Tenderloin," because the kickbacks they received there paid them enough to afford steak for dinner.

In the early 1970s, the 41st Precinct police station in the Bronx earned its nickname on a chaotic evening when an arrow with a wig attached ended up on a lieutenant's desk. After a local resident used a bow and arrow to kill a wig-stealing intruder and while crowds stormed the precinct to protest a question-able arrest, desk lieutenant Lloyd Gittens glanced at the scalp-like evidence and referred to his precinct as Fort Apache, and the name stuck.

Budget cuts may have reduced the N.Y.P.D. by 4,000 officers in the last ten years, but of the 210 American cities with a population of at least 100,000, New York City ranks 194th (with No. 1 being the worst) in terms of crime.

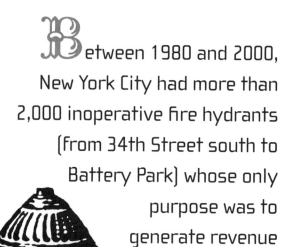

etween 1980 and 2000, New York City had more than 2,000 inoperative fire hydrants (from 34th Street south to Battery Park) whose only purpose was to generate revenue in parking fines.

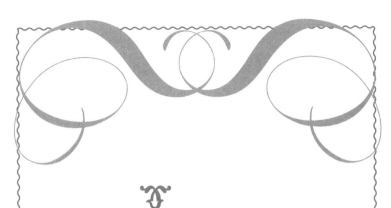

In 1993,
more than half of
the residents of
Staten Island voted
to secede from
New York City.

Alec Hoag was a New York City thief and con man who pulled off countless scams thanks to a pair of police officers who provided protection in exchange for a piece of the pie. However, when Hoag tried to cheat the cops out of their share of the loot, they turned around and beat him at his own game—and "Smart Alec" (as they sarcastically called him) ended up in jail. Eventually, the name became generic for any obnoxious know-it-all.

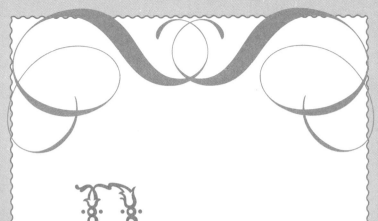

onald Trump's first major real estate deal was converting the Commodore Hotel, next to Grand Central Station, into the Grand Hyatt in 1980.

The most expensive real estate in New York City just may be the sidewalk underneath the pushcart on the south side of the front steps of the Metropolitan Museum of Art. Given the vendor's yearly license fee of approximately $350,000 for a space that is approximately four by eight feet, that would break down to a cost of over $10,000 a square foot.

The original American Express card was introduced in New York City in 1958. For the first year, it was made of paper, not plastic— and for the first eleven years, it was purple, not green.

One of the highest priced single purchases ever charged to an American Express card was in 1994 at a Sotheby's New York auction, when Los Angeles art collector Eli Broad bought Roy Lichtenstein's painting, "I ... I'm Sorry," for $2.5 million and paid for it with plastic. The purchase entitled Broad to 2.5 million frequent flyer miles.

New York City zip code 10021, on Manhattan's Upper East Side, has generated more money for presidential candidates than any other zip code in the country.

In Manhattan, for a $5,500 fee, and with the approval of the Borough President's office, buildings can be issued a "vanity address." This explains why a building that does not front an avenue (most commonly Park, Madison, or Fifth) is able to use (and financially benefit from) a prestigious avenue address.

Throughout the nineteenth century, it was tradition for crowds to gather around the bell tower of Trinity Church to literally ring in the New Year. In 1904 the celebration moved to Times Square in midtown, newly renamed in honor of the new 42nd Street headquarters of the *New York Times*. On December 31, 1904, the paper marked the start of the new year with a rooftop, midnight fireworks display.

In 1908, New York City officials banned the shooting of fireworks over the heads of a crowd, so Adolph Ochs, the publisher of the *New York Times*, turned to a long-standing time-telling device used by the Naval Observatory. Just as a time ball positioned on a mast atop a building dropped daily to mark the noon hour, Ochs dropped an illuminated iron ball, perched on the roof of the twenty-five-story Times building, at midnight to mark the start of 1909.

The first crossword puzzle appeared as a "word-cross" in the *New York World* in 1913. It was an instant hit, and years later, when the aunt of Columbia University graduate Richard Simon wondered why no one published a book of puzzles, Simon and his friend Max Schuster launched a company to do exactly that. It took almost another twenty years after Simon & Schuster built an empire on the success of a single volume of crosswords for the *New York Times* to start publishing them.

The largest Sunday edition of the *New York Times* was delivered on September 14, 1987; it was 1,612 pages and weighed twelve pounds.

Charles Dow, the financial reporter who founded *The Wall Street Journal* and created the Dow Jones Industrial Average, never graduated from high school.

ollegiate School,
an all-boys school at 78th
Street and West End Avenue,
was founded in 1628, making
it the oldest school in the
United States.

Manhattan College is in the Bronx and Long Island University is in Brooklyn.

Lombardi's in Little Italy began selling pizza in 1905 for 5 cents a pie. The establishment, originally a grocery store, is credited as the country's first pizzeria and was located a few doors down from the Lombardi's open today at 32 Spring Street.

With an inventory of over 50,000 garments, 4,000 shoes, 300,000 fabric swatches (grouped thematically for visual reference), and 1,300 sample books, the museum at the Fashion Institute of Technology houses the largest permanent collection of costumes, accessories, textiles, and apparel in the world.

In 1900, 22-year-old electronics whiz Joshua Cowen designed a miniature electric railroad car and sold it to Robert Ingersoll, a toy retailer, as "window dressing" to attract attention to his Manhattan store. Although the first person who saw the moving display was indeed lured into the shop, he wanted to buy the train rather than the merchandise it featured. When Ingersoll ordered more, Cowen incorporated, taking his middle name—Lionel—for the new business venture.

The sight of vendors on every corner of Manhattan baking pretzels under a row of heat lamps inspired Kenner Toys to create the kid-friendly Easy-Bake Oven, which is heated by a 100-watt light bulb.

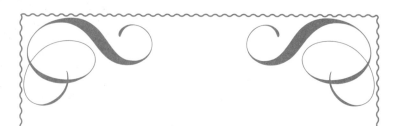

When married NYU art students Harry and Patricia Kislevitz noticed that the vinyl they were using for a school project adhered to the semigloss paint in their bathroom, they decorated the walls with cutout vinyl shapes. They had so much fun adding to and rearranging the giant collage that they scaled down the idea to create a design toy they called Colorforms.

T he small numbers after each letter in the 35th Avenue street sign (on the corner of 81st Street) in Jackson Heights, Queens, are meant to resemble Scrabble tiles. The game was invented there in the early 1940s by architect Alfred Butts, who tested and refined it at the Community United Methodist Church on that block.

To protect themselves from the British, the Dutch built a palisade wall across the northern boundary of New Amsterdam in 1653. When a road was built that followed the line of the wall it became known as Wall Street.

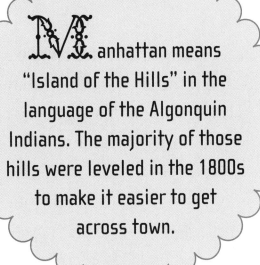

Manhattan means "Island of the Hills" in the language of the Algonquin Indians. The majority of those hills were leveled in the 1800s to make it easier to get across town.

Since 2001, people have sent more post-cards of New York's World Trade Center than of any other building in the world.

In the wake of a yellow fever epidemic of the early nineteenth century, a canal was dug in lower Manhattan so that the contents of a contaminated pond near what is now City Hall could be drained into the Hudson River. The canal was later filled in, and the resulting thoroughfare is called Canal Street.

600,000

manhole covers in New York City

300 POUNDS

weight of an individual manhole cover

150 DEGREES

average temperature of New York City
pavement on a hot summer day

500 FEET

legally required distance, according
to city zoning, between a strip club
and a school

20

"short blocks"—traveling north
or south—to a mile

To take in all the sights along Broadway, from beginning to end, would require traveling more than 321 miles. Broadway starts at Bowling Green (a park in the financial district), and runs 17 miles through Manhattan, continuing for another 4 miles through the Bronx, then into Westchester County—where it becomes Route 9—along the eastern bank of the Hudson River and nearly all the way to the Canadian border.

The black spots visible on sidewalks all over New York City, usually taken to be part of the concrete mix or remnants of roofing tar that dripped, are actually discarded pieces of chewing gum that have hardened and, over time, become embedded in the pavement.

120

"chewing gum spots" per
sidewalk square in heavily
traversed areas of
New York City

Dr. Seuss's first book, *And To Think That I Saw It on Mulberry Street*, was rejected twenty-seven times before he stepped into a midtown office elevator and bumped into an old friend who happened to be working at a publishing house. The Mulberry Street that Seuss wrote about, however, is not the one in lower Manhattan, but rather, the Mulberry Street found in his hometown of Springfield, Massachusetts.

Kay Thompson based her popular *Eloise* children's books on her own godchild—Liza Minnelli.

Edna St. Vincent Millay, the first woman to receive the Pulitzer Prize for poetry, gained her middle name from St. Vincent's hospital in Manhattan, where her uncle's life had been saved shortly before her birth.

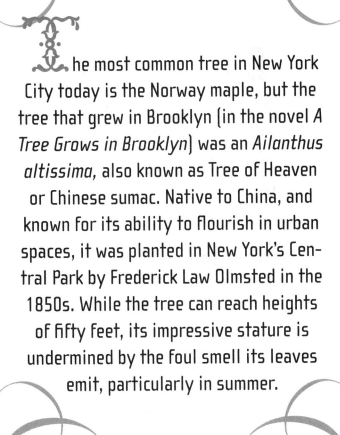

The most common tree in New York City today is the Norway maple, but the tree that grew in Brooklyn (in the novel *A Tree Grows in Brooklyn*) was an *Ailanthus altissima*, also known as Tree of Heaven or Chinese sumac. Native to China, and known for its ability to flourish in urban spaces, it was planted in New York's Central Park by Frederick Law Olmsted in the 1850s. While the tree can reach heights of fifty feet, its impressive stature is undermined by the foul smell its leaves emit, particularly in summer.

ockingbirds traditionally mimic the sounds and songs of other birds, but mockingbirds living in New York City have been known to imitate police sirens, car alarms, buses, and the beeping of garbage trucks being driven in reverse.

he Algonquin Hotel has had a cat in the lobby since the 1930s, when a stray wandered in and the hotel's owner let him stay. According to lore, that cat routinely drank milk out of a champagne glass, and impressed with these theatrics, actor John Barrymore took to calling him Hamlet. Today, male Algonquin cats are called Hamlet; if female, they go by Matilda. (No one seems to know where that name came from.)

By the Numbers

4

zoos in New York City

6

public ice rinks in
New York City

550

public tennis courts in
New York City

15

public golf courses in
New York City

In the late 1920s, there were more than 150 miniature golf courses built and operating on rooftops in New York City. The country was in the height of the Depression, and bankers and brokers in particular would use them as a way to relieve stress.

No one really knows who invented the first bra, but Manhattan socialite Mary Phelps Jacobs, who improvised an undergarment out of two handkerchiefs and pink ribbon, was the first to patent one. Unfortunately, the bra company Jacobs created could not sustain itself, and she bailed, happily selling the rights to her design for $1,500. Ouch. Years later, that design would come to be worth $15 million.

Over 10,000 books have been written about New York City. Add one more to the list.

DISCLAIMER

All facts, figures, statistics, stories, quotes, and anecdotes found on these pages were checked (and double-checked) and believed to be true (or have some semblance of truth) at the time the book went to press. But things change; stuff happens. So cut me some slack if they're not.

ABOUT THE AUTHOR

David Hoffman is a television writer, a frequent on-camera correspondent, and the author of over a dozen books about popular culture, for which, in recent years, he has been paid to play with toys, challenge untapped cooking skills (with the help of some big-name chefs), and eat and shop his way across the country. He lives in Los Angeles, where he likes to pretend this is hard work.

ABOUT THE AUTHOR

David Hoffman is a television writer, a frequent on-camera correspondent, and the author of over a dozen books about popular culture, for which, in recent years, he has been paid to play with toys, challenge untapped cooking skills (with the help of some big-name chefs), and eat and shop his way across the country. He lives in Los Angeles, where he likes to pretend this is hard work.